Christmas
Designs Coloring Book

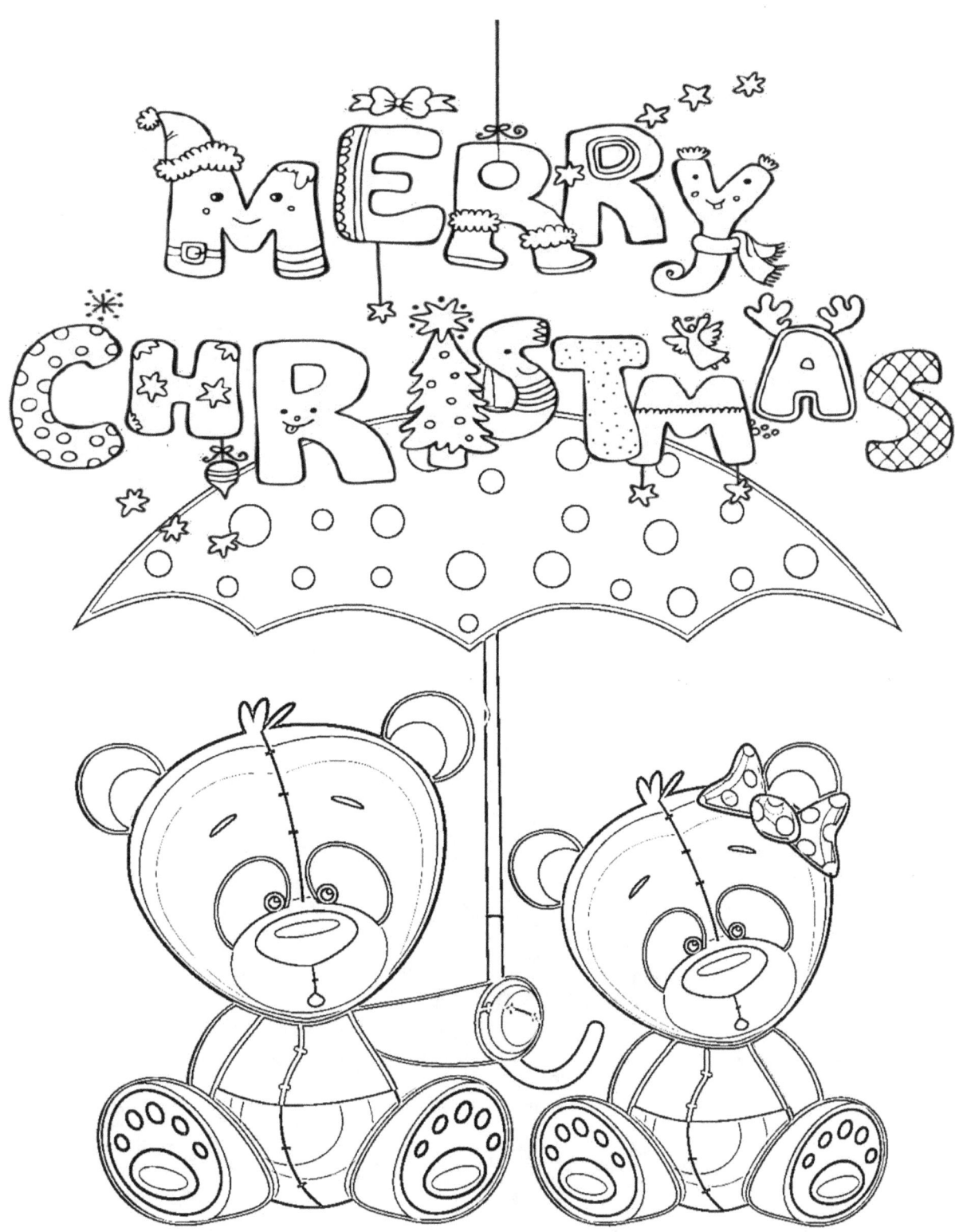

Merry Christmas

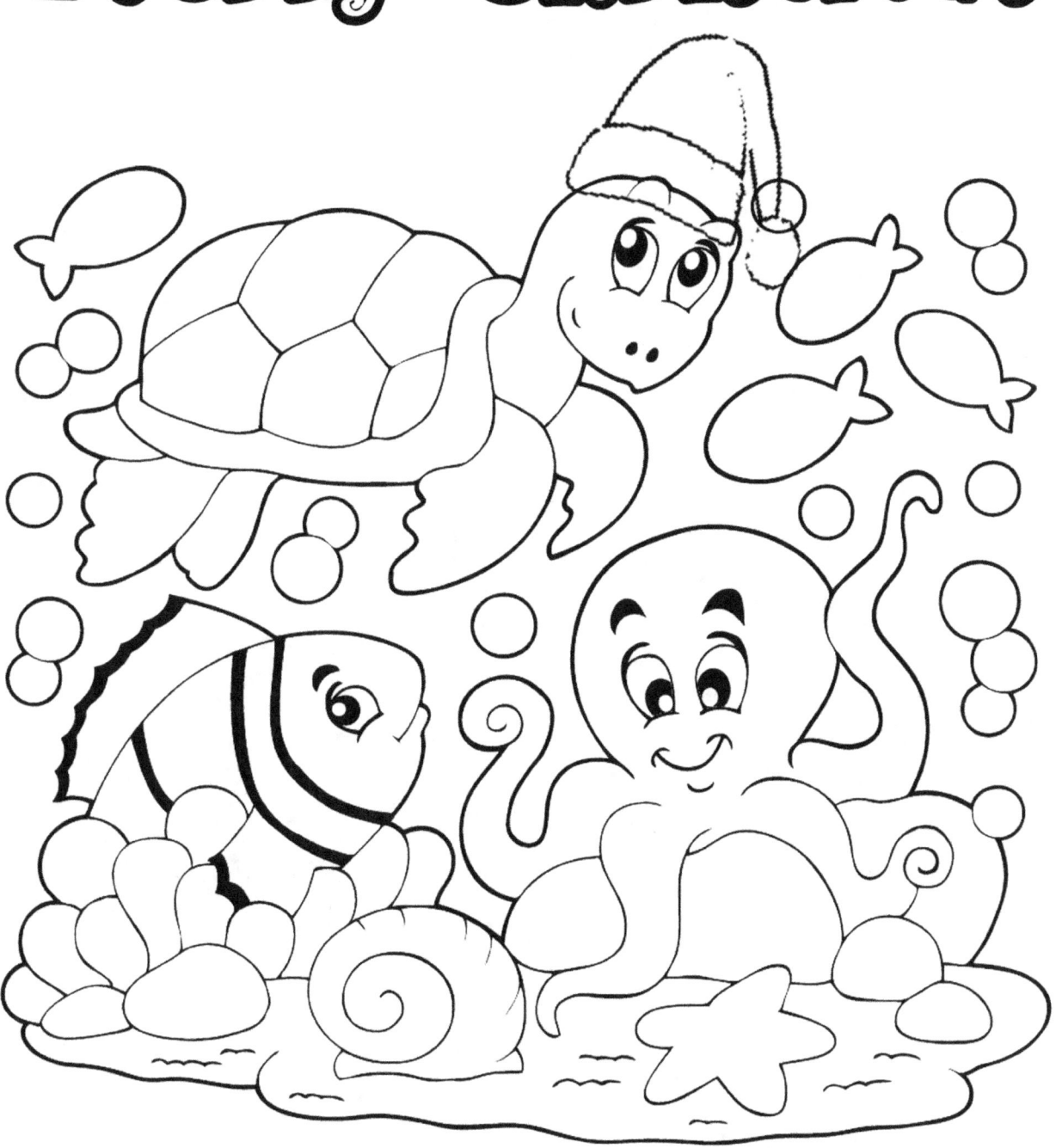

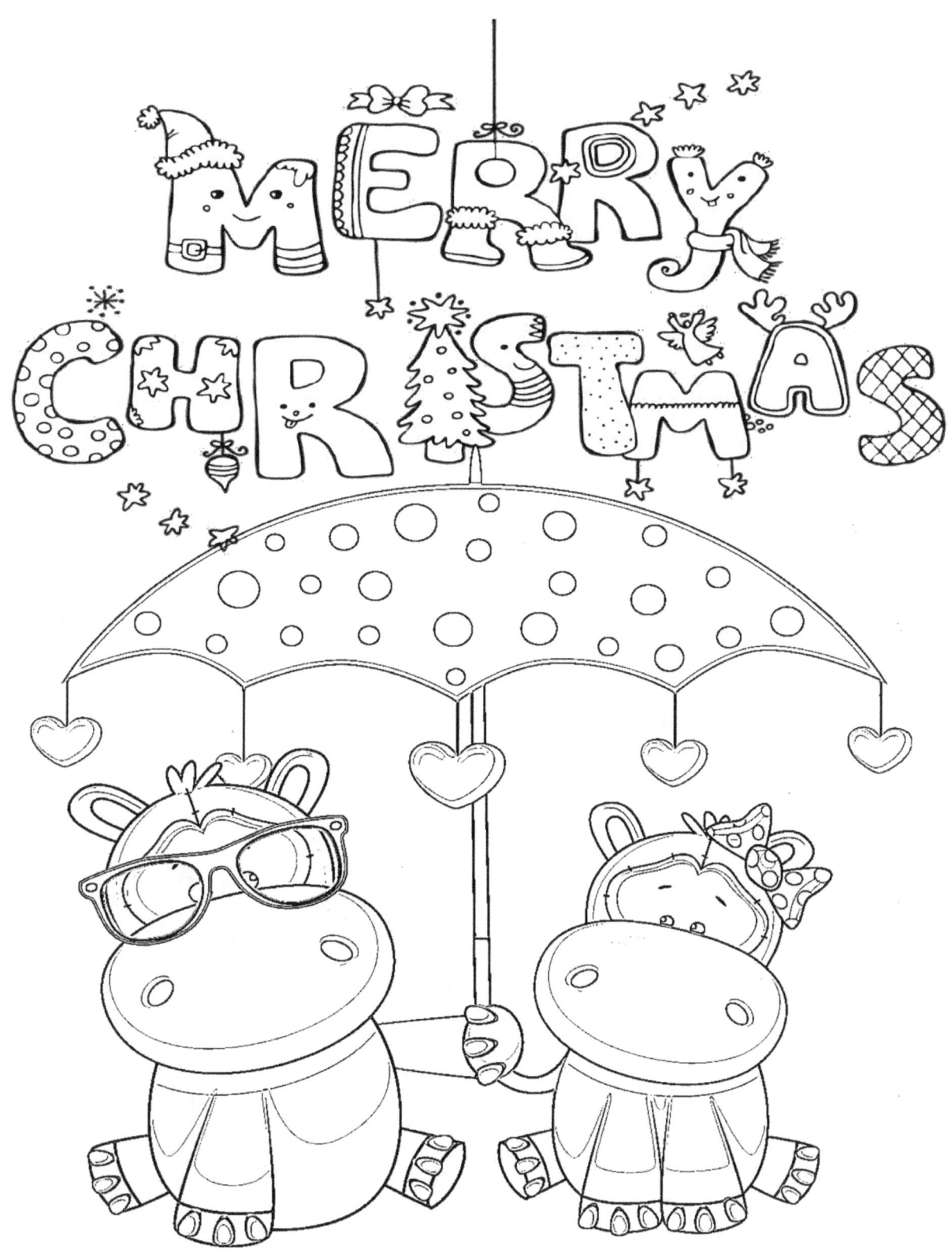

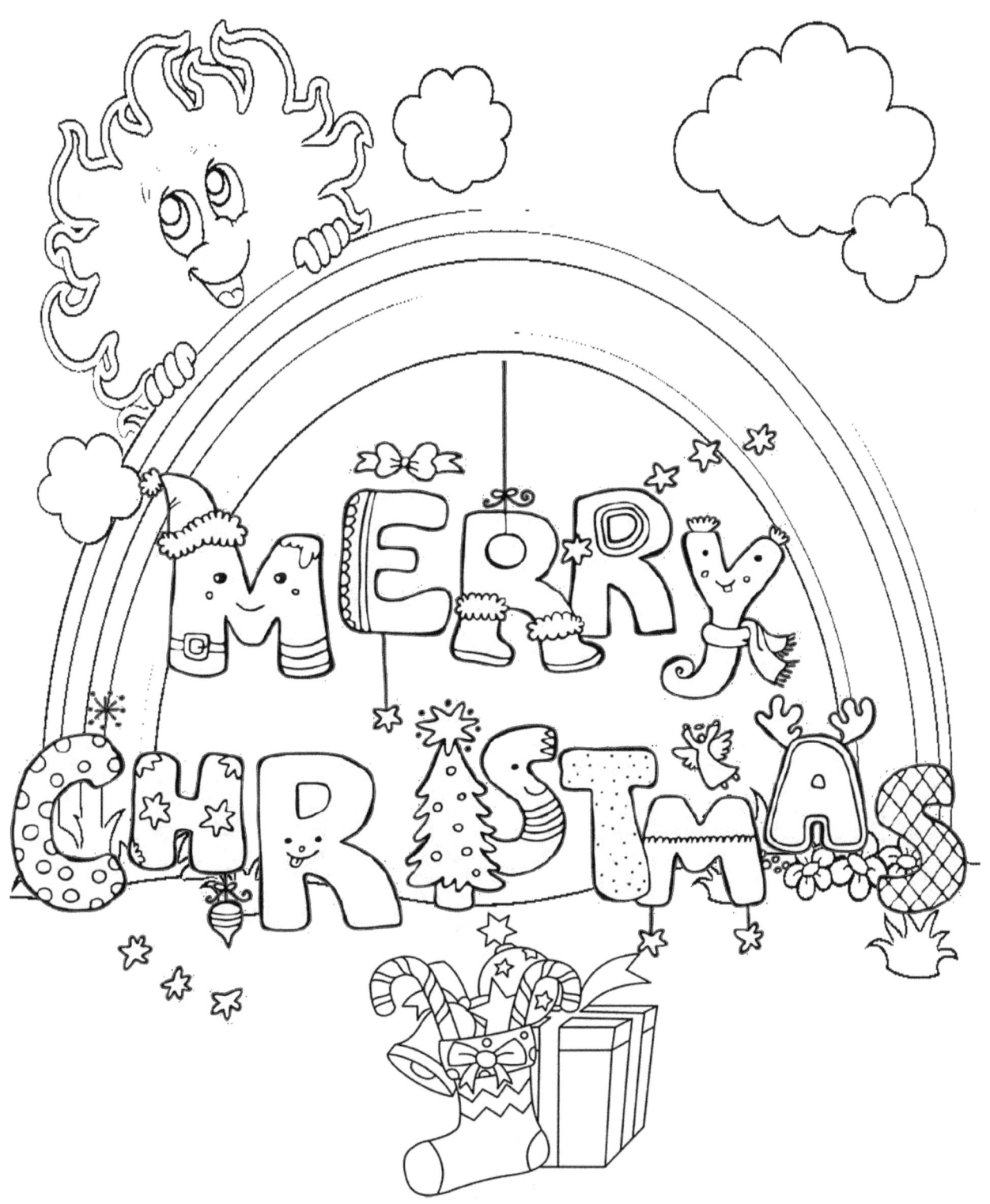

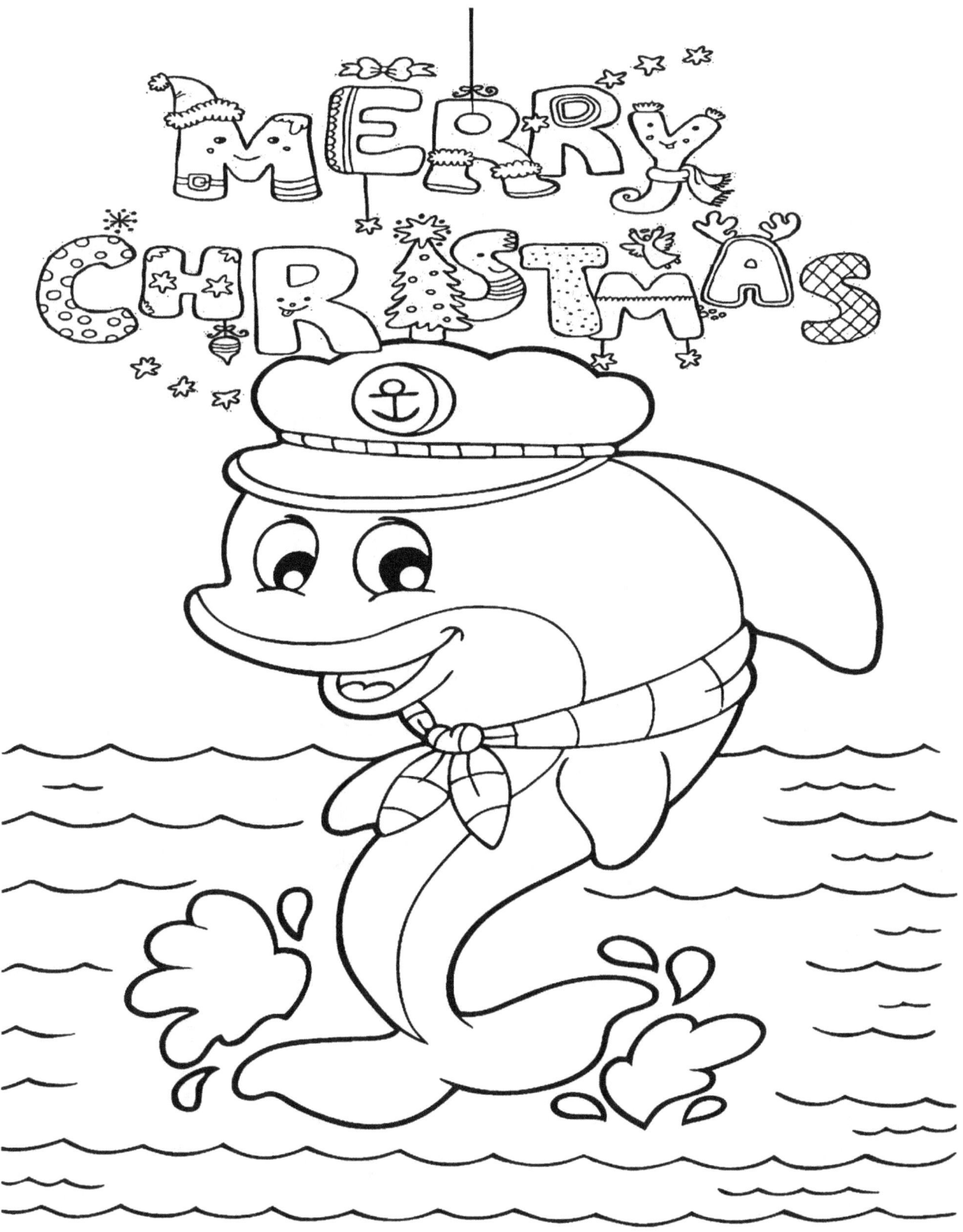

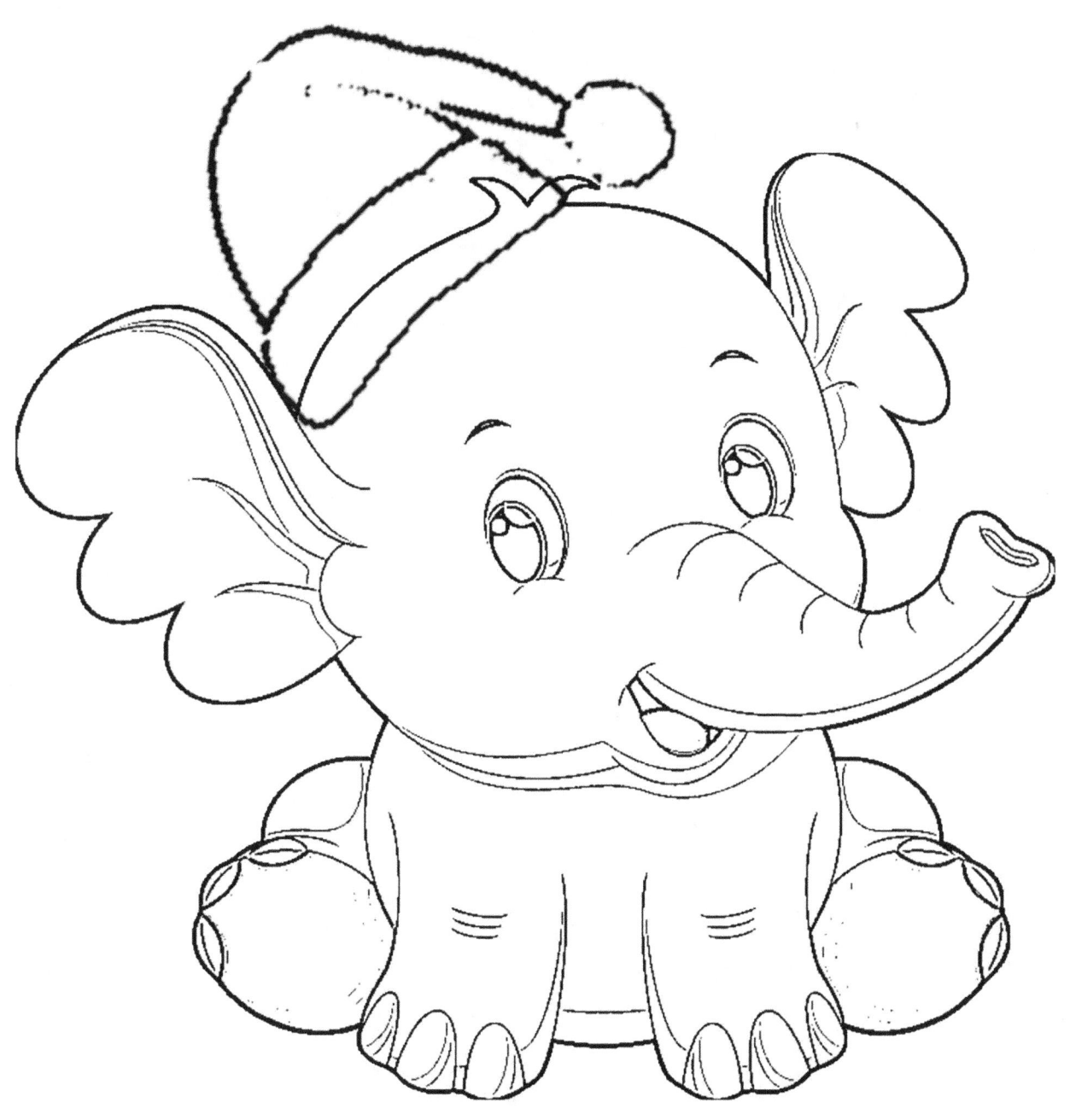

Merry Christmas

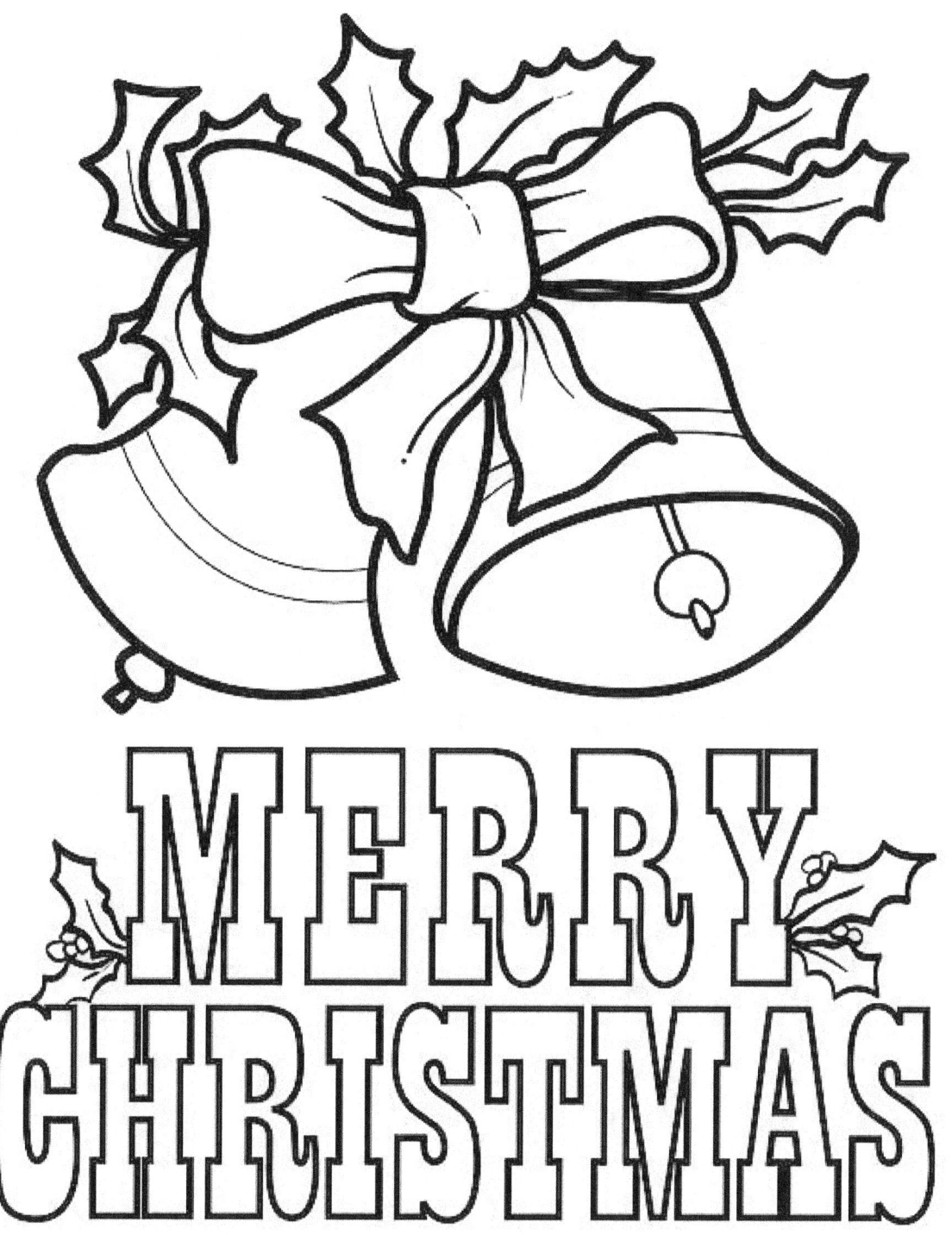

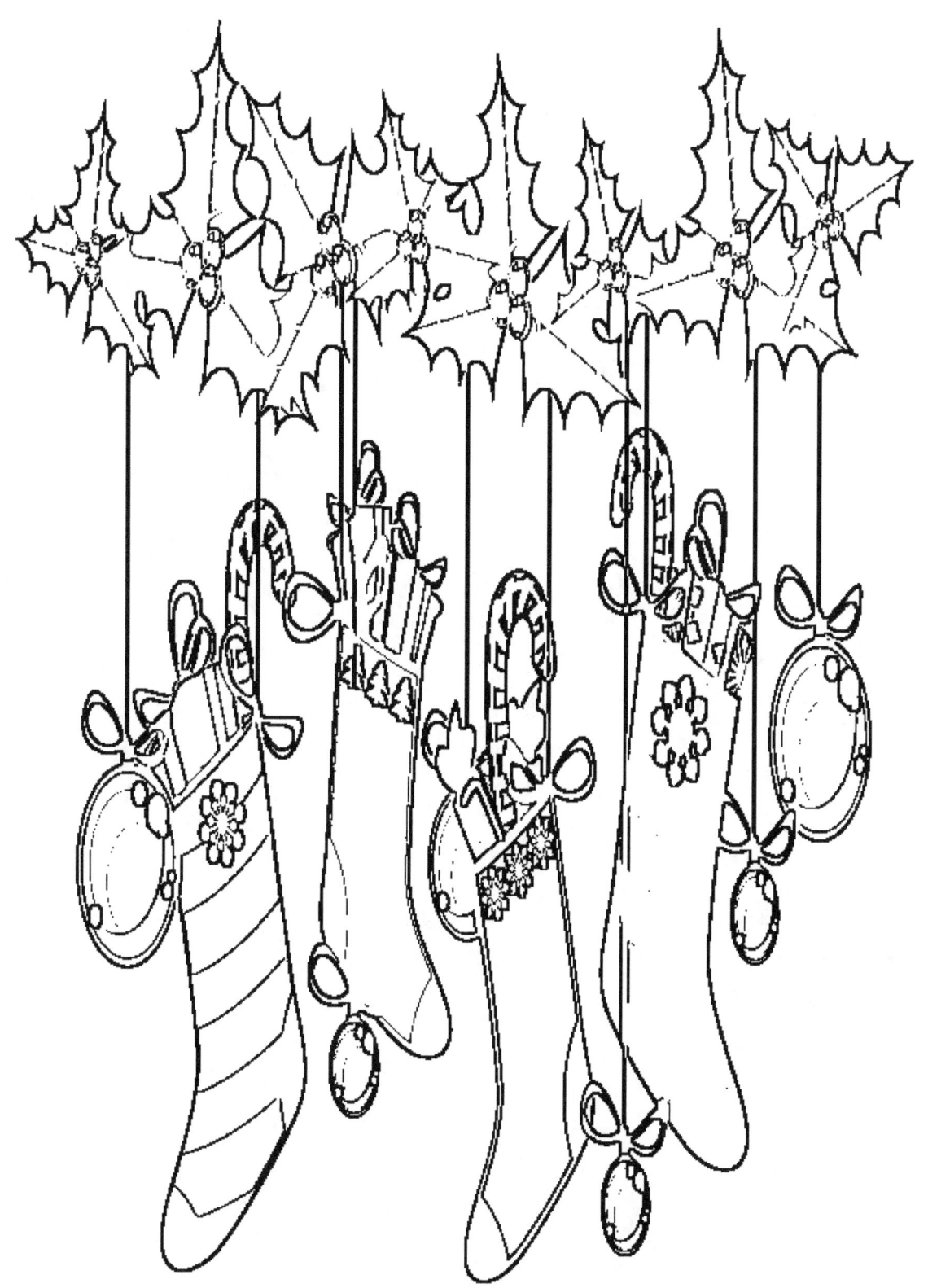

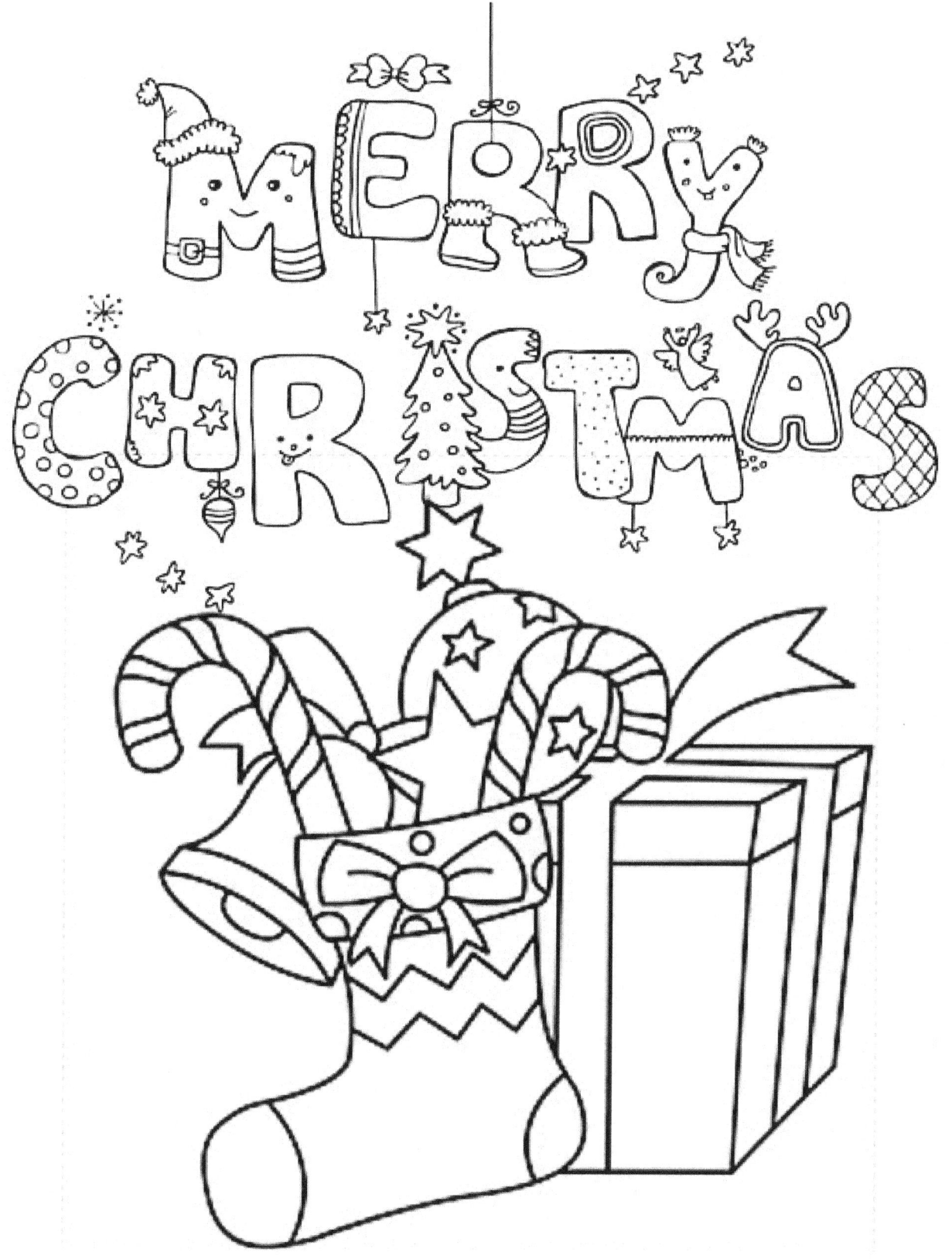

MERRY CHRISTMAS

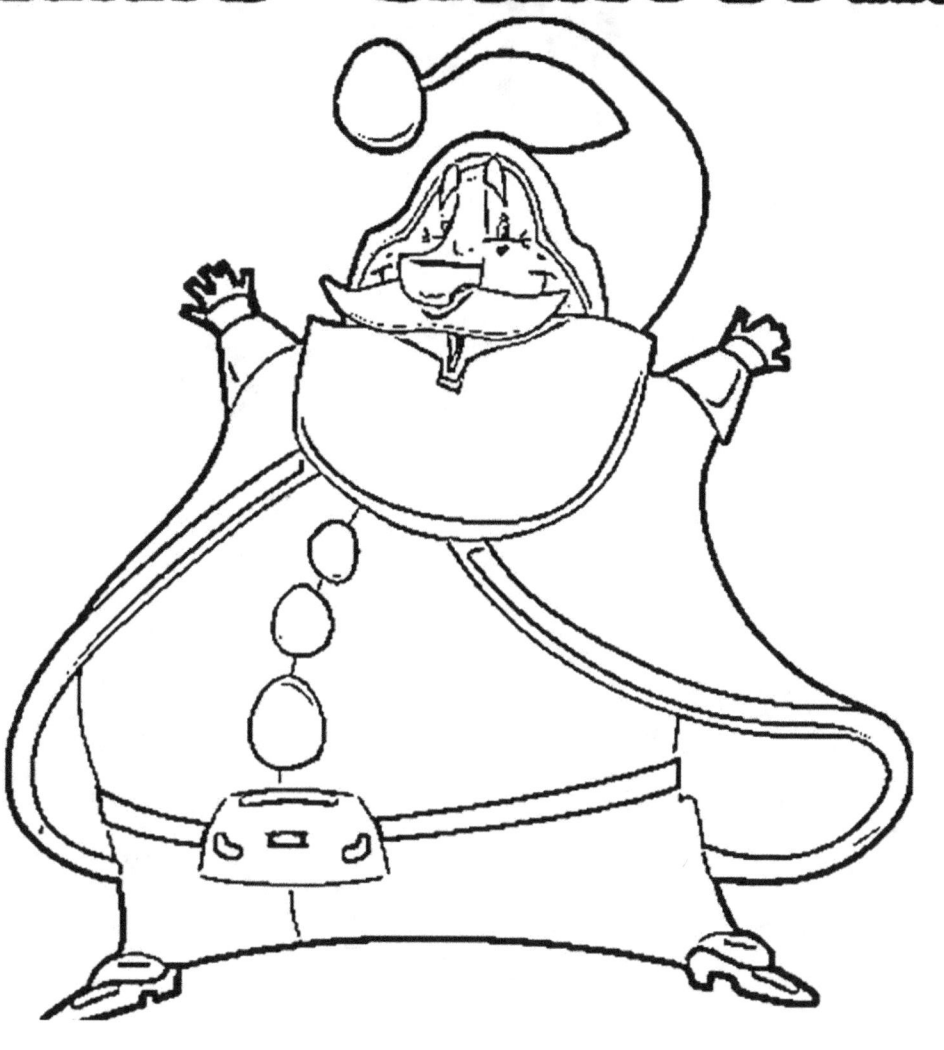

Merry Christmas

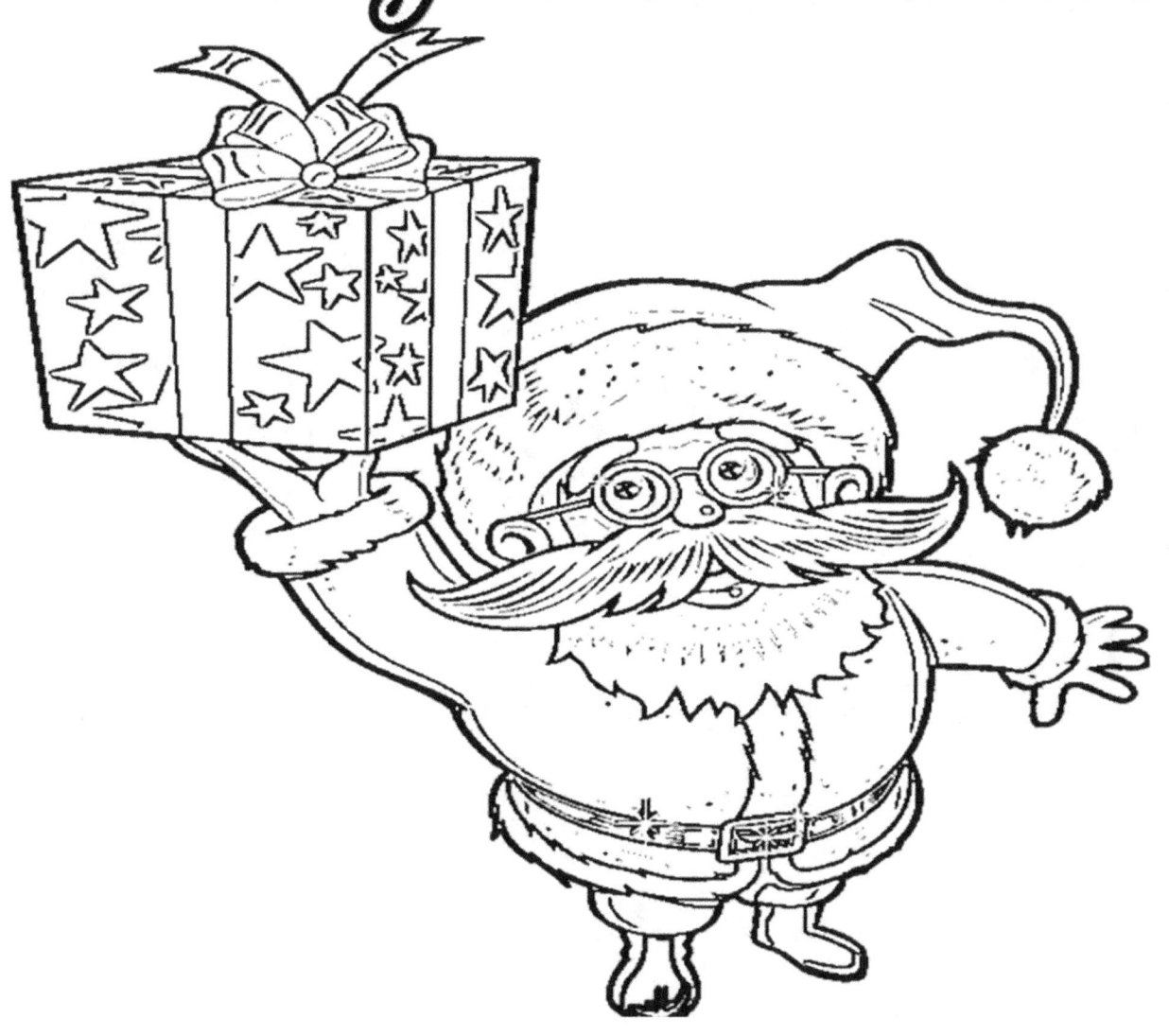

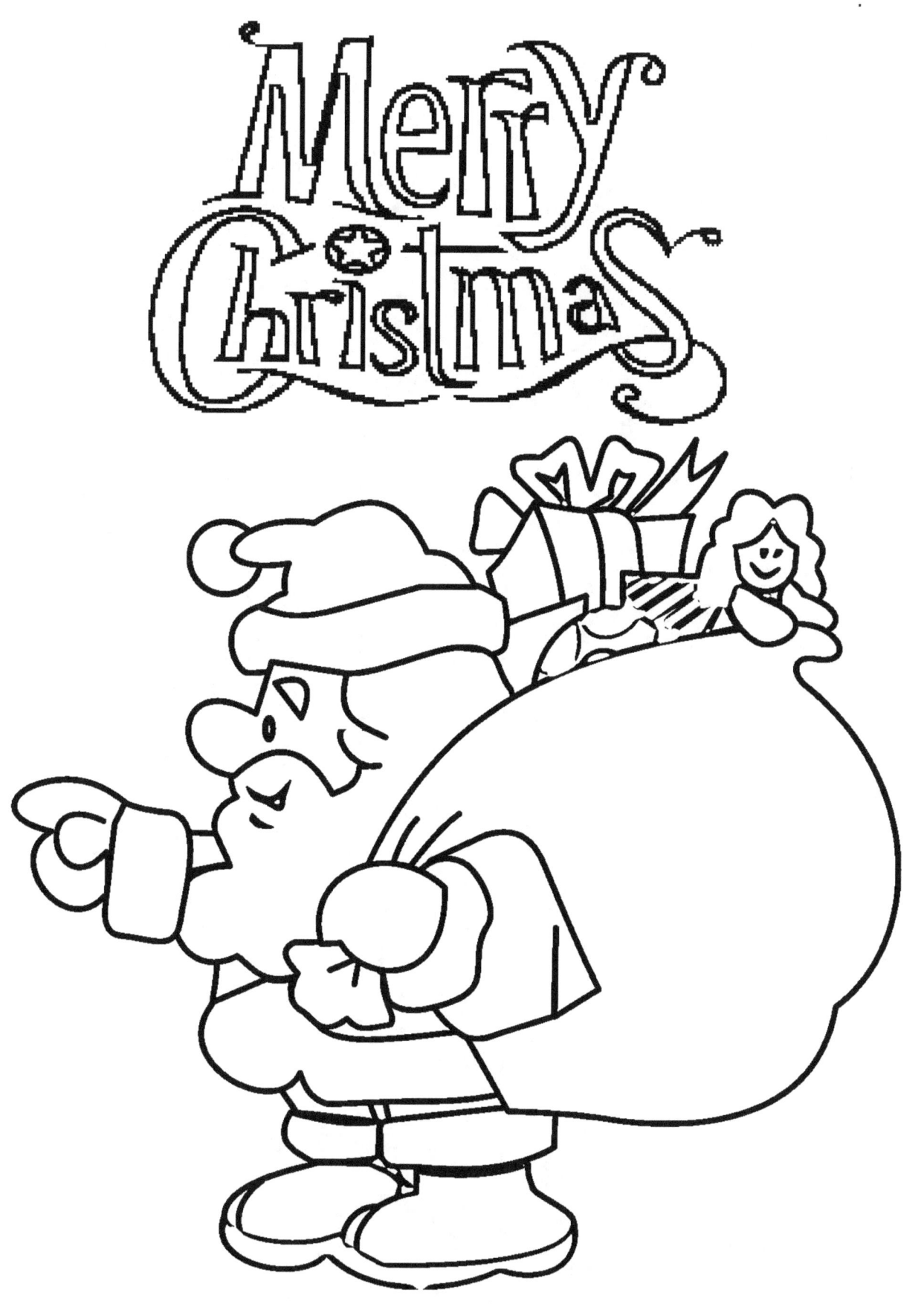

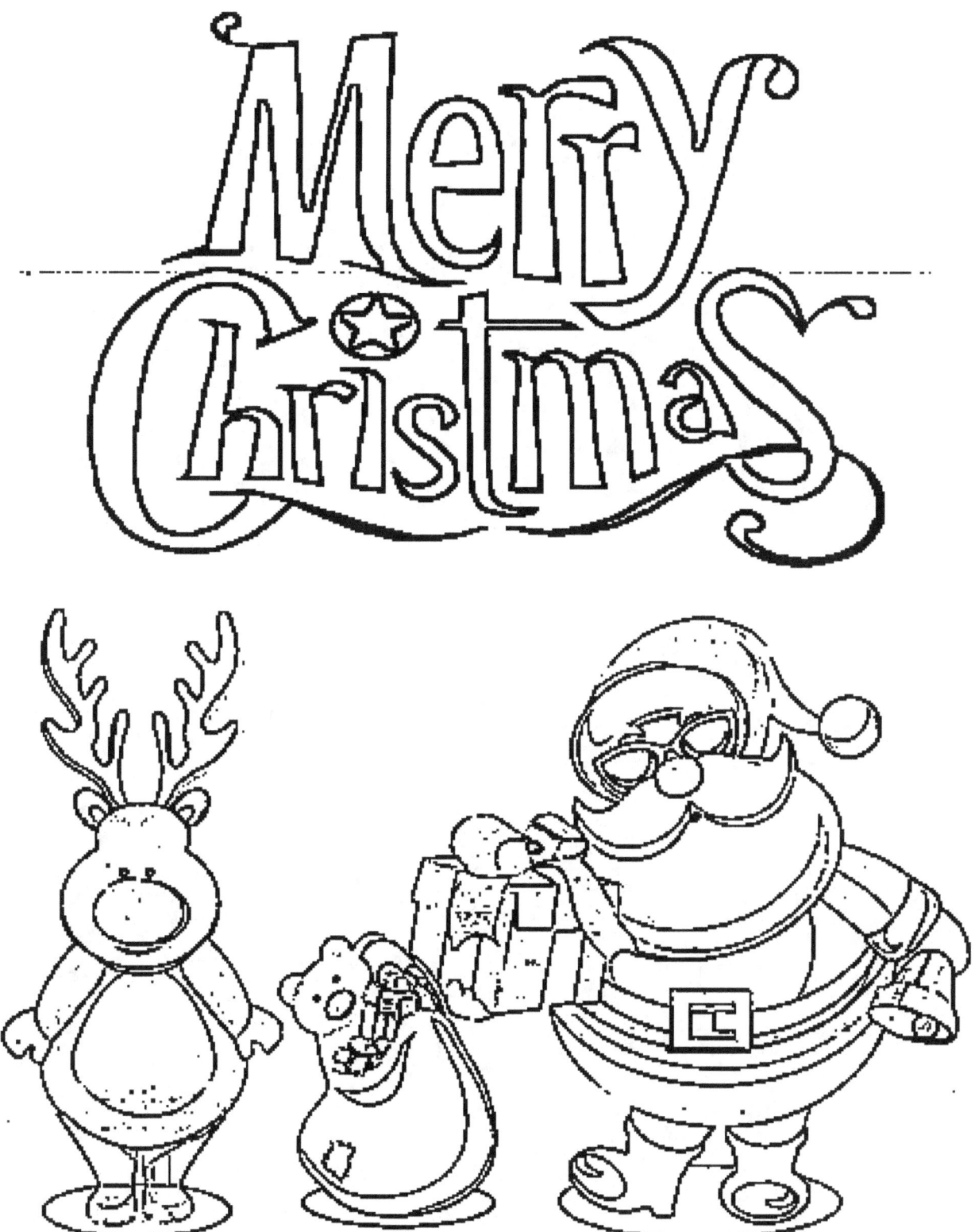

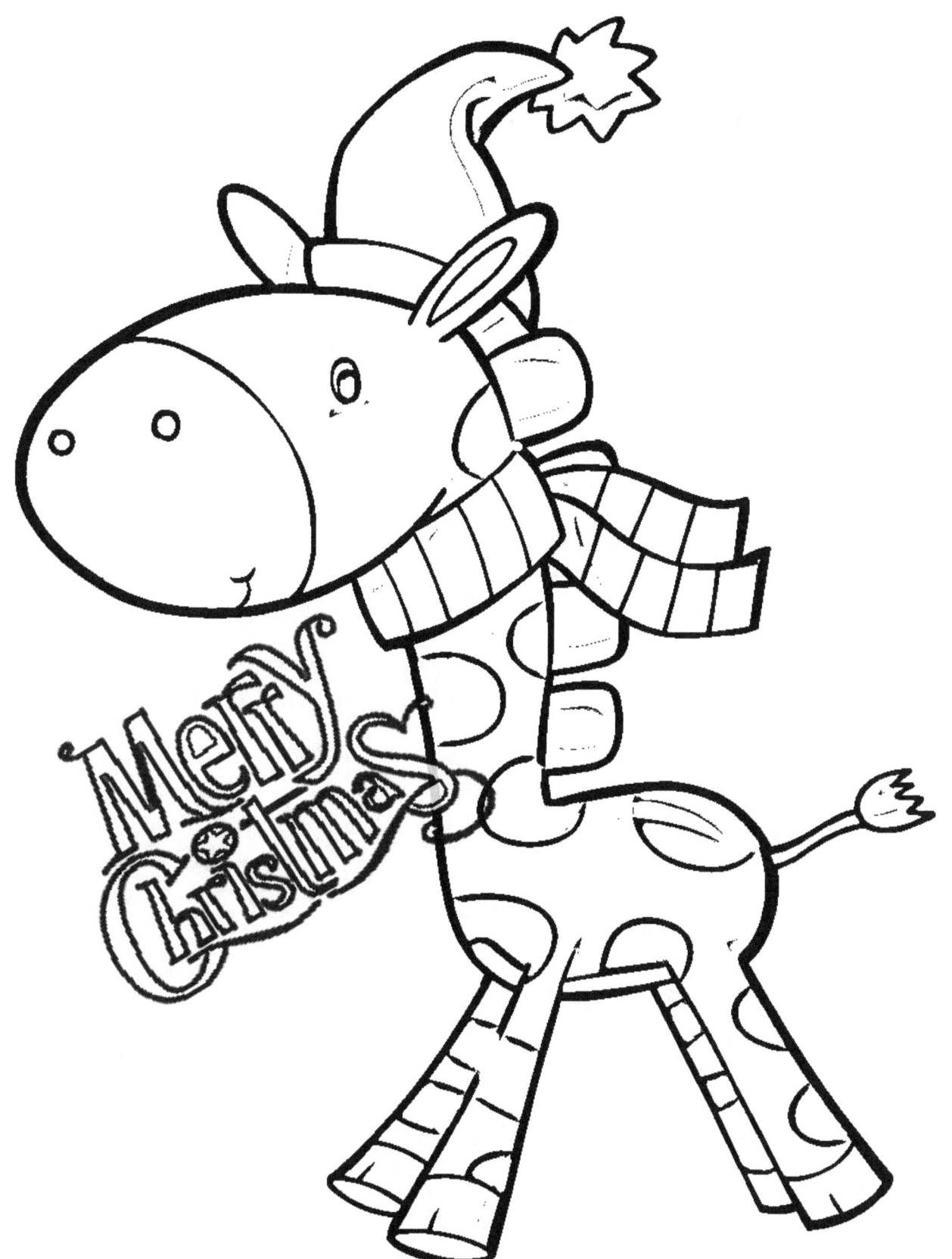

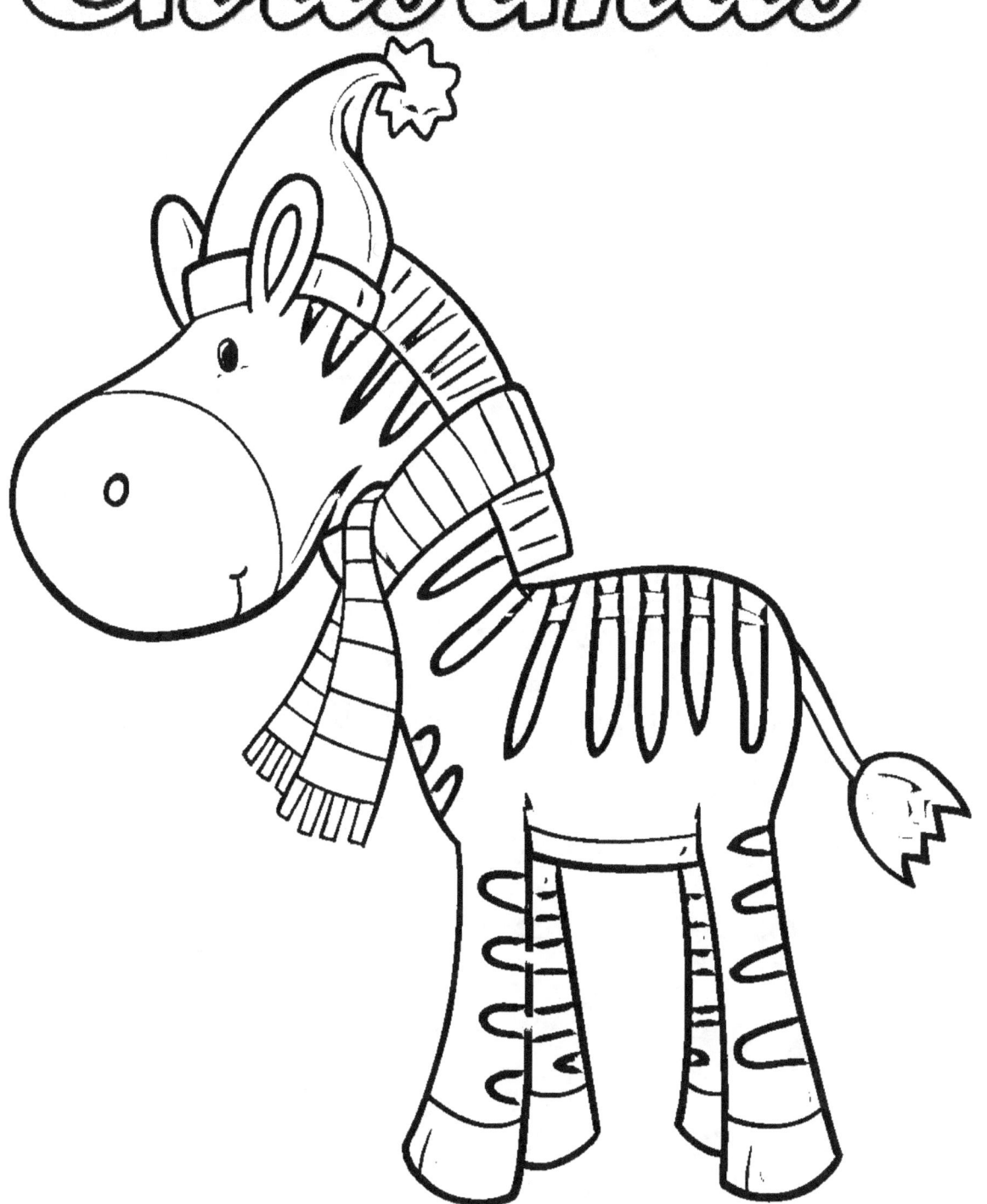

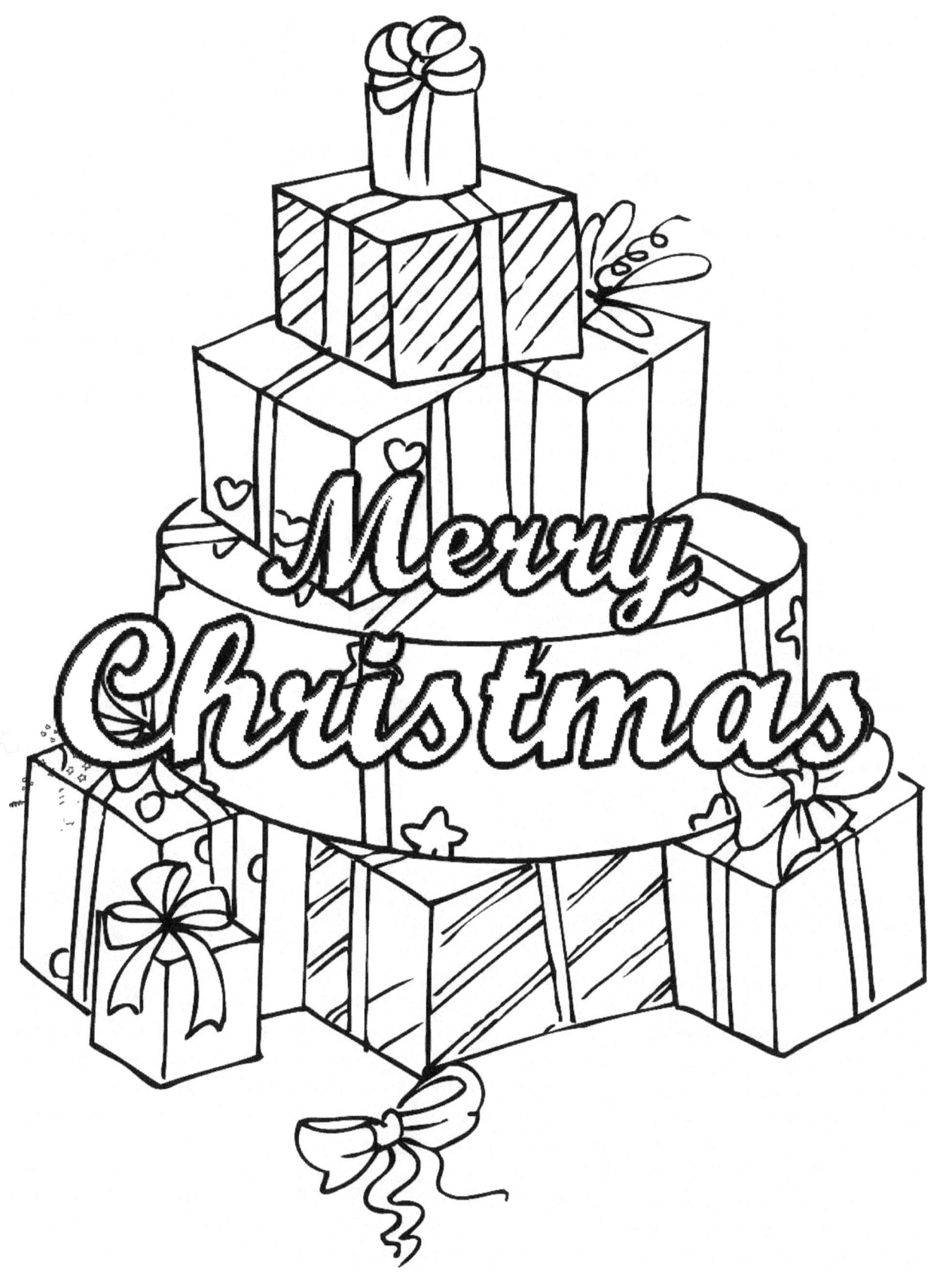

Merry Christmas

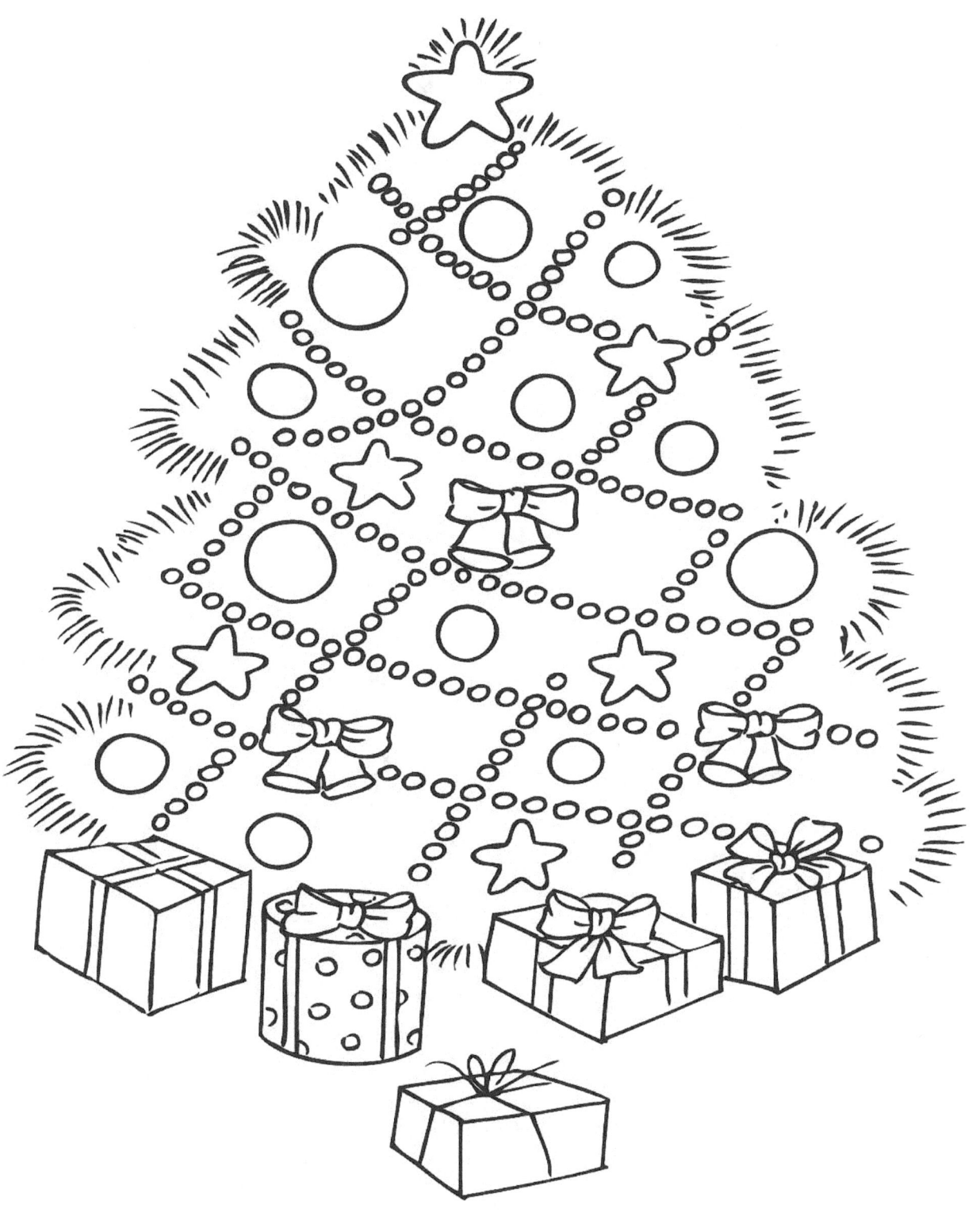

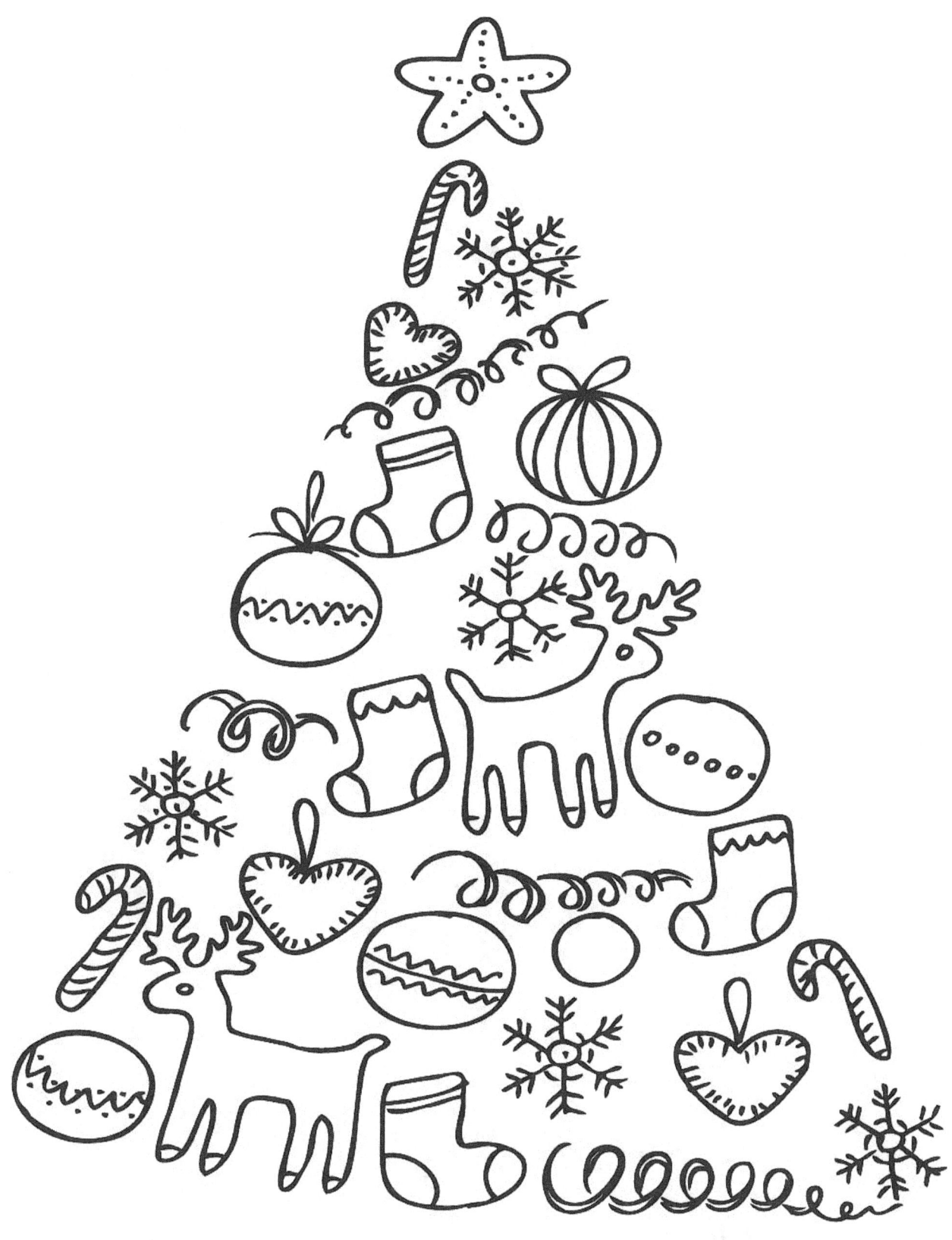

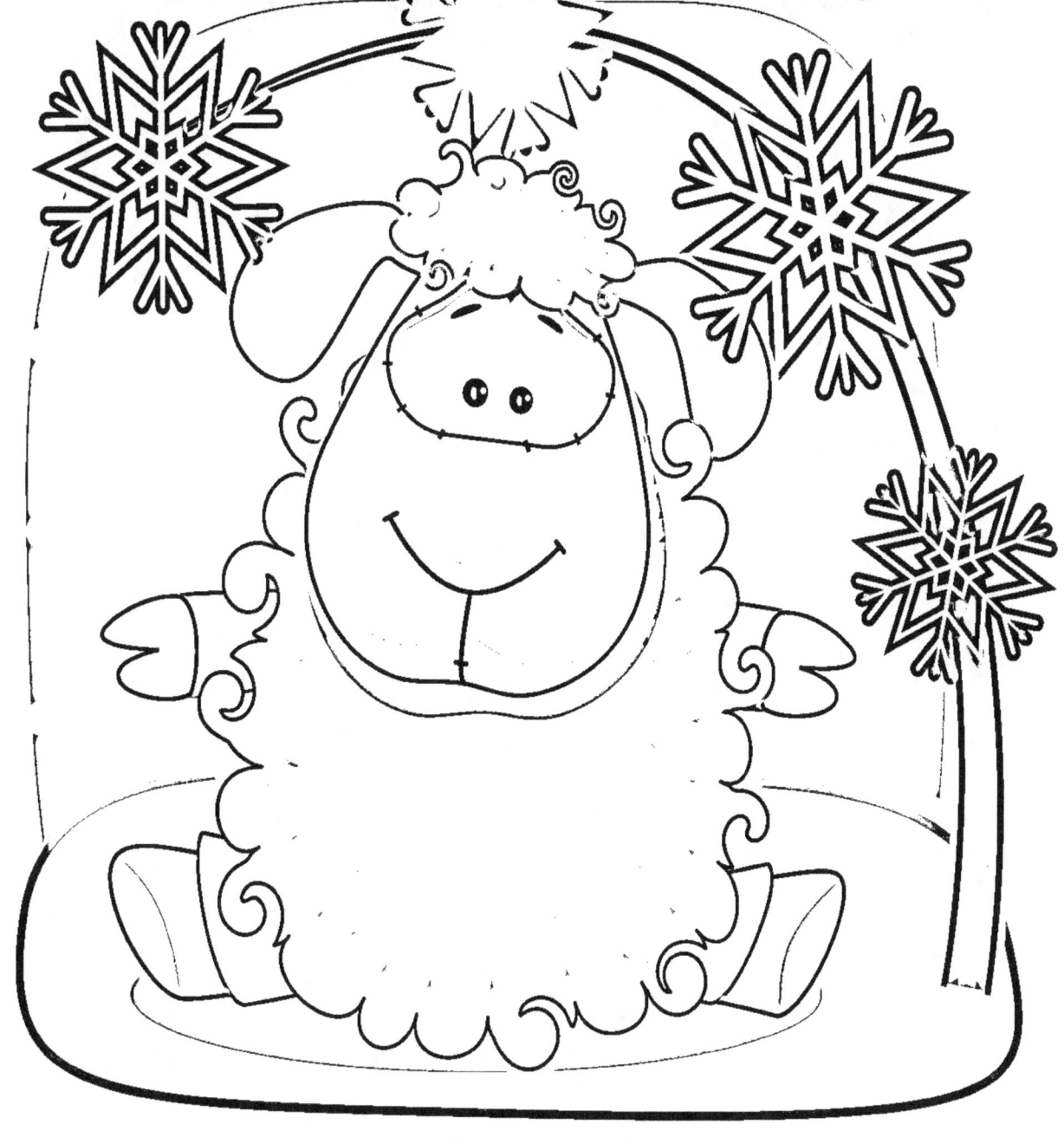

Merry Christmas

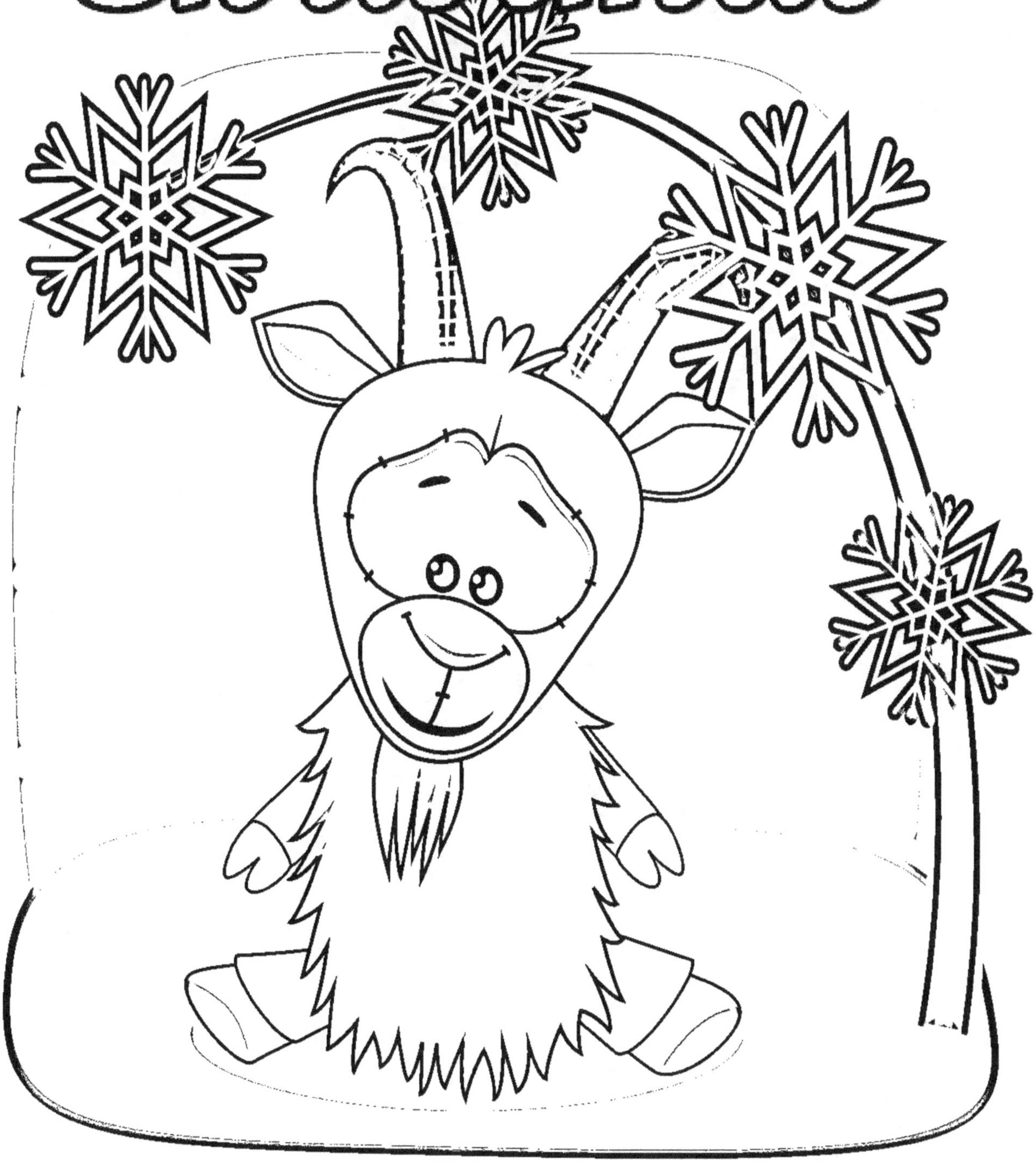

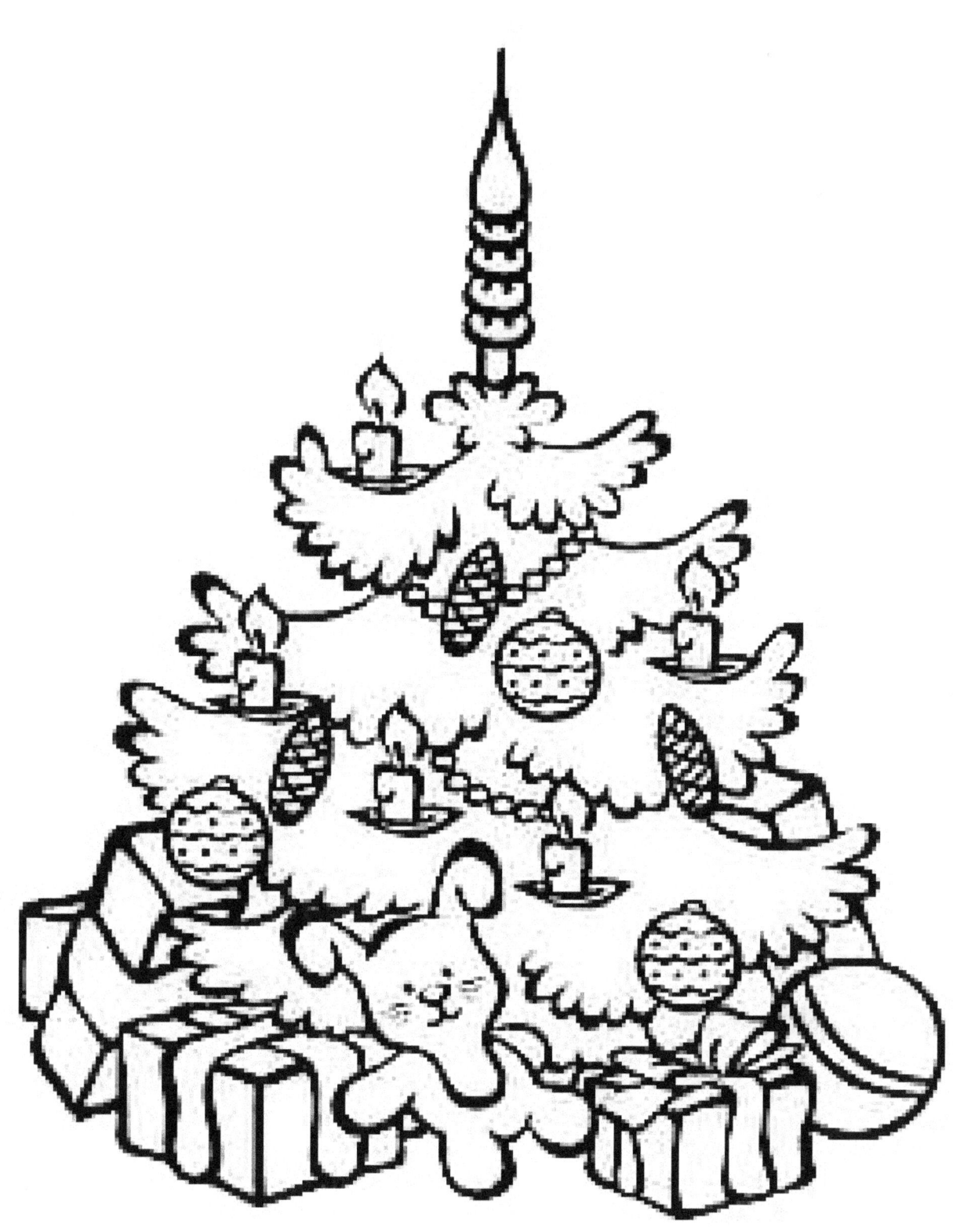

Merry Christmas

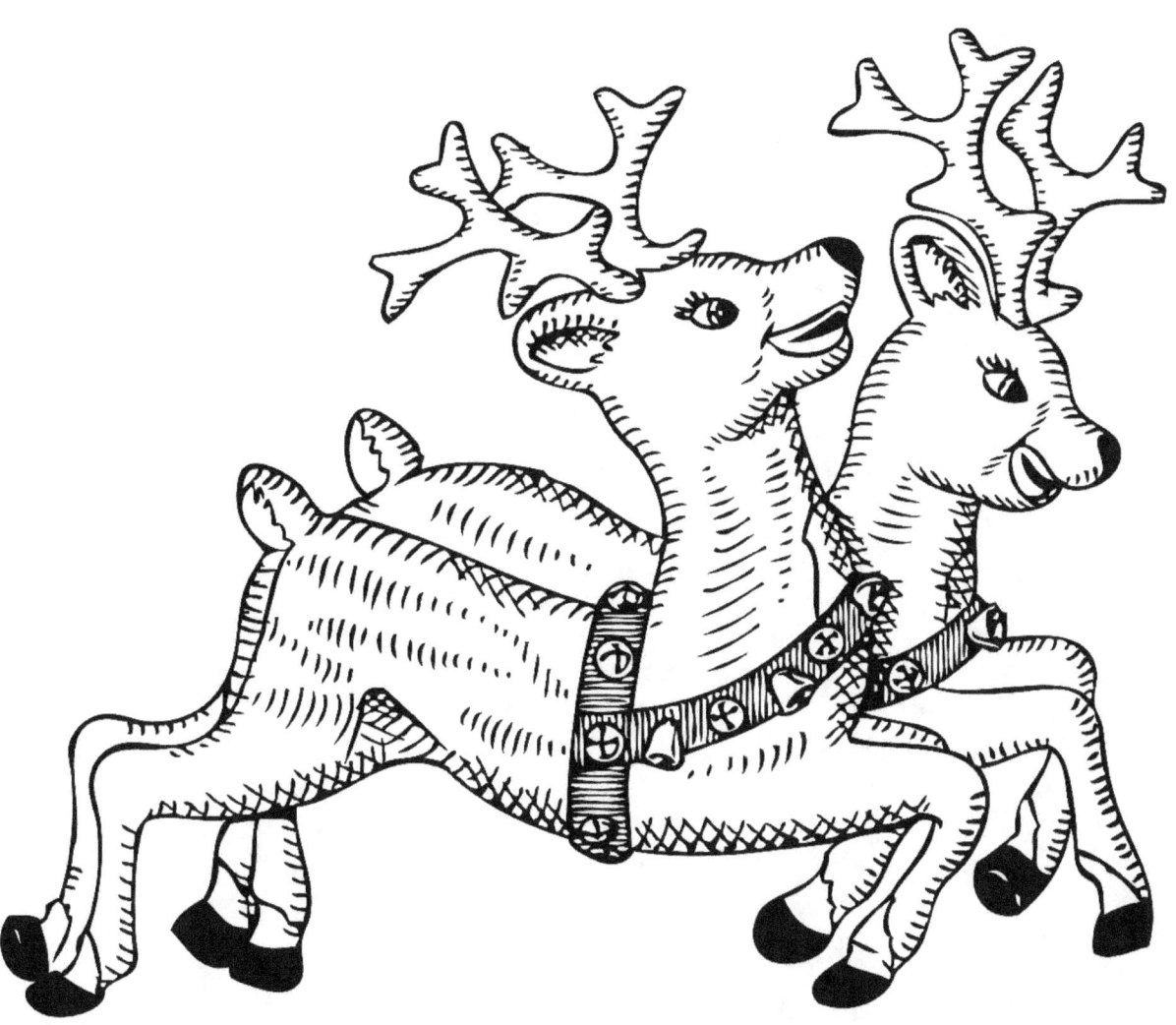

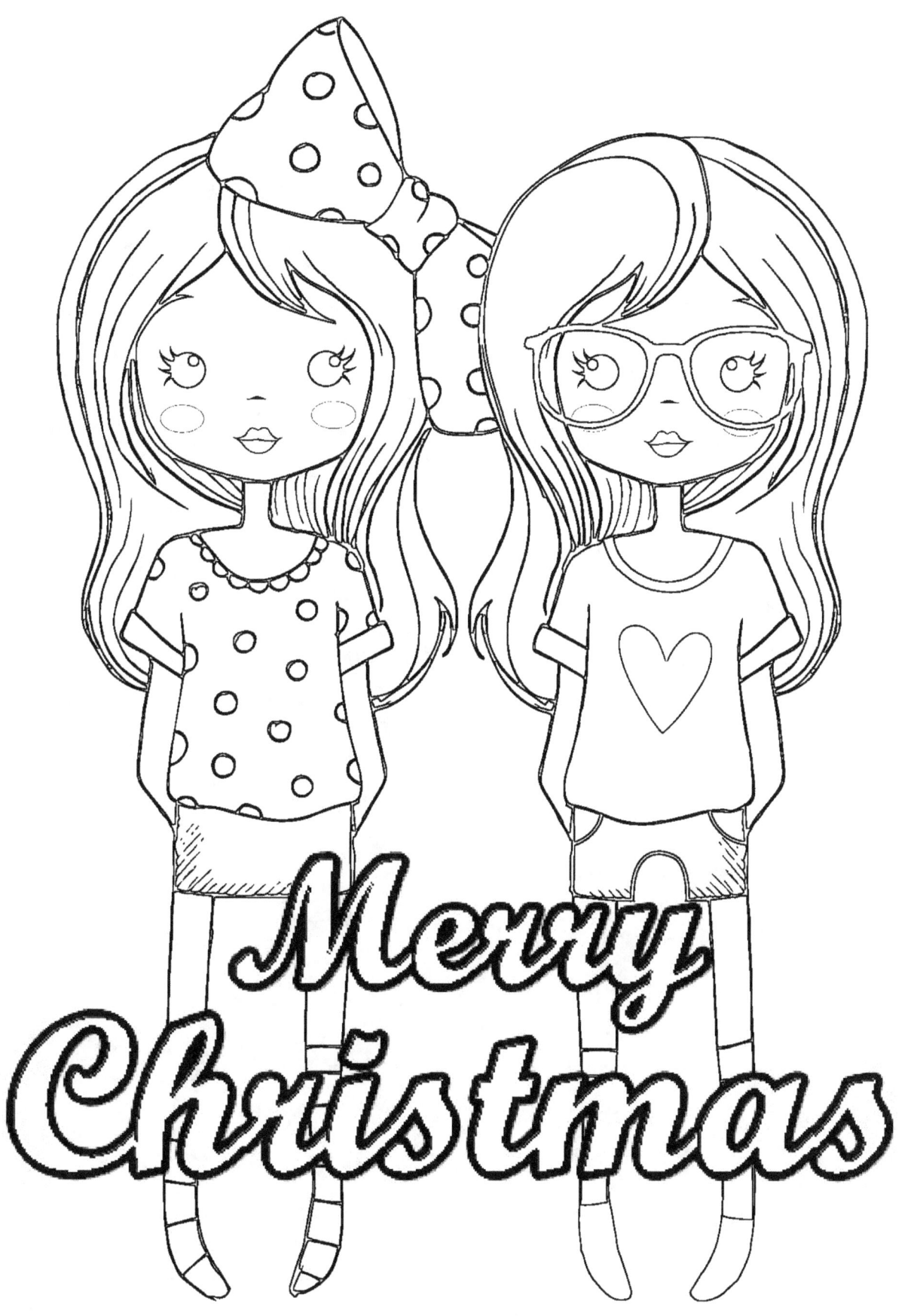

Merry Christmas

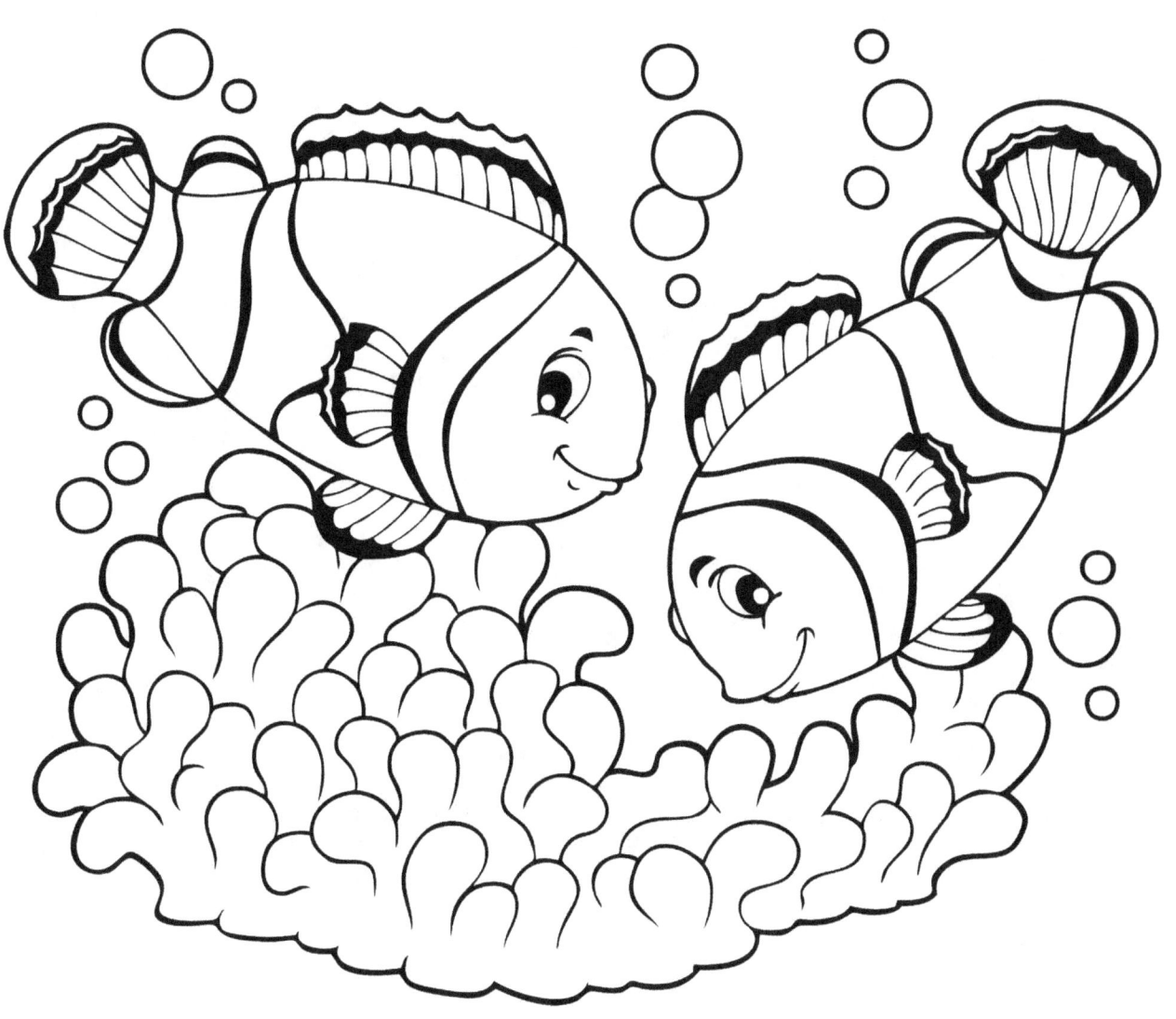

www.ingramcontent.com/pod-product-compliance
Lightning Source LLC
Chambersburg PA
CBHW081621170526
45166CB00009B/3061